GEGE AKUTAMI

Hamburger!!!

GEGE AKUTAMI published a few short
works before starting *Jujutsu Kaisen*, which began
serialization in *Weekly Shonen Jump* in 2018.

JUJUTSU KAISEN

VOLUME 14
SHONEN JUMP MANGA EDITION

BY GEGE AKUTAMI

TRANSLATION **Stefan Koza**
TOUCH-UP ART & LETTERING **Snir Aharon**
DESIGN **Joy Zhang**
EDITOR **John Bae**
CONSULTING EDITOR **Erika Onabe**

JUJUTSU KAISEN © 2018 by Gege Akutami
All rights reserved.
First published in Japan in 2018 by SHUEISHA Inc., Tokyo.
English translation rights arranged by SHUEISHA Inc.

The stories, characters, and incidents mentioned
in this publication are entirely fictional.

Printed in Italy

Published by VIZ Media, LLC
P.O. Box 77010
San Francisco, CA 94107

10 9 8 7 6 5
First printing, February 2022
Fifth printing, August 2024

viz.com

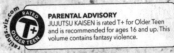

JUJUTSU KAISEN

14

THE SHIBUYA INCIDENT
—RIGHT AND WRONG—

STORY AND ART BY GEGE AKUTAMI

**Jujutsu High
First-Year**

Yuji Itadori

—CURSE—

Hardship, regret, shame… The misery
that comes from these negative human
emotions can lead to death.

On October 31, cursed spirits seal off Shibuya
and ensnare Gojo. As the jujutsu sorcerers
frantically try to rescue Gojo, Toji Zen'in
bursts in and defeats Dagon, allowing
Fushiguro and the others to return from
Dagon's domain. However, soon after their
return, Jogo's flame burns Nanami, Maki, and
Naobito. A curse user severely wounds
Fushiguro, and Toji kills himself. Meanwhile,
Yuji Itadori has been fed numerous fingers,
and Sukuna has awakened. He squares off
against Jogo, who summons help…

**Special Grade
Cursed Object**

Ryomen
Sukuna

Jujutsu High
First-Year

**Megumi
Fushiguro**

Jujutsu High
First-Year

Nobara Kugisaki

Special Grade
Jujutsu Sorcerer

Satoru Gojo

Grade 1
Jujutsu Sorcerer

Kento Nanami

JUJUTSU KAISEN

14

THE SHIBUYA INCIDENT —RIGHT AND WRONG—

HANAMI.

DAGON.

SORRY.

B WOO...

...IS STILL ALIVE.

MAHITO...

HOWEVER, *HUMANS* LINGER BEYOND IT AS WELL.

DEATH IS SOMETHING *HUMANS* FEAR AND DETEST.

DEATH IS A MIRROR FOR *HUMANS.*

MAHITO IS THAT MIRROR.

MAHITO WILL CONTINUE TO GROW STRONGER.

THAT'S WHY YOU...

...PROPPED HIM UP AS THE LEADER.

...

WHEN WE'RE REBORN, WE WON'T BE THE SAME AS BEFORE.

EVEN SO, I'LL BE ANTICIPATING THE DAY WE MEET AGAIN.

WE'RE THE...

...TRUE HUMANS.

SO YOU WANTED TO...

...BECOME HUMAN?

NOT BECOMING A HUMAN *LITERALLY*. MORE LIKE TAKING THEIR PLACE, RIGHT?

YEAH, YEAH... I KNOW WHAT YOU MEAN.

...IT MAKES IT ALL THE MORE FOOLISH.

THAT SAID...

COMPARING THEMSELVES TO THOSE AROUND THEM...

...LEADS TO WEAKNESS AND STUNTS THEIR GROWTH.

HUMANS FLOCKING TOGETHER. CURSES FLOCKING TOGETHER.

BUT YOU LACKED THE *HUNGER* TO TAKE HOLD OF YOUR DESIRES.

TO REACH THE HEIGHTS OF SATORU GOJO AND NOT WORRY ABOUT YOUR FUTURE OR IDENTITY.

YOU SHOULD HAVE BURNT EVERYTHING YOU DESIRED TO A CINDER.

YOU'RE...

...PROBABLY RIGHT.

BUT YOU KNOW...

...THIS WAS ACTUALLY FUN WHILE IT LASTED.

HUMANS. JUJUTSU SORCERERS. CURSED SPIRITS.

YOU'RE NOT BAD COMPARED TO THOSE I FOUGHT OVER THE LAST THOUSAND YEARS.

STAND
PROUD.

DON'T ASK ME.

I DON'T KNOW WHAT THAT IS EITHER.

MASTER SUKUNA.

THMP

KRAKL
KRAKL

I'VE COME TO ESCORT YOU.

WHO ARE YOU?

THE 2020 VALENTINES RANKINGS THAT I SERIOUSLY ALMOST FORGOT

> PROBABLY RIGHT AROUND WHEN THE PAST ARC ENDED.

RANKINGS (VALENTINES RECEIVED)	CHARACTER	AKUTAMI'S COMMENT
1 (54)	GOJO	OKAY, I GET IT ALREADY...
2 (30)	GETO	NOT TOO BAD.
3 (23)	FUSHIGURO	YOU NEED TO TRY A LITTLE HARDER.
4 (22)	ITADORI	SQUEAKING BY AS THE MAIN CHARACTER.

JUJUTSU KAISEN

THE *TEN SHADOWS TECHNIQUE* BEGINS WHEN...

...A SORCERER RECEIVES TWO DIVINE DOGS.

...THE SORCERER AND THEIR DIVINE DOGS MUST EXORCISE THEM TOGETHER.

IN ORDER TO USE OTHER SHIKIGAMI...

...TO EXORCISE AND AMASS EVEN MORE SHIKIGAMI. UP TO TEN.

THEN THE SORCERER GAINS MORE SHIKIGAMI, WHICH THEY CAN UTILIZE...

...

ARE YOU FINISHED YET?

THAT GIRL FROM BEFORE WAS PRETTY STRONG TOO. AND ALL OF YOU ARE STILL SO YOUNG.

11:05 P.M.
DOGENZAKA,
IN FRONT OF SHIBUYA 109

SEE?

BUT WITH ALL THAT BLEEDING, I PROBABLY WON'T EVEN NEED TO—

EVEN THOUGH HE'S ON HIS LAST LEGS, HE ISN'T GIVING ME AN OPENING TO GET CLOSE.

YEESH.

THUD

FOR THE SORCERER, IT'S A POINTLESS EXORCISM.

?

BUT EVEN A POINTLESS EXORCISM HAS ITS USES.

BUT DOING SO NULLIFIES THE TECHNIQUE'S EFFECT AFTER THE EXORCISM IS DONE.

NGH

THE THING IS...YOU CAN EXORCISE A SHIKIGAMI WITH MULTIPLE PEOPLE.

DO YOU KNOW WHY THE GOJO AND ZEN'IN FAMILIES ARE ON BAD TERMS?

THEY'RE ON BAD TERMS?

THE WORST.

RRRMBBBBB

!!

THAT DOESN'T MEAN I CAN BECOME STRONGER THAN YOU.

...USED IT THIS WAY TOO.

I.BET THE HEAD OF THE HOUSEHOLD...

YOU DONE?

BLAH BLAH BLAH BLAH.

SHK SHK

AN EARTH-QUAKE?

GWOOO

HEH HEH...

WOW, SO WHO'S THE SHOWOFF?

YOU CAN'T USE A SHIKIGAMI UNLESS YOU EXORCISE IT.

PLZZT

LET ME CONTINUE.

...IN ORDER TO **EXORCISE** THEM.

...CURSED ENERGY?!

WHAT IS THIS...

BUT YOU CAN SUMMON THEM ANYTIME YOU WANT...

...HAS EVER BEEN ABLE TO EXORCISE THIS ONE.

NOT A SINGLE USER OF THE TEN SHADOWS TECHNIQUE ...

NGH "THE THING IS... YOU CAN EXORCISE A SHIKIGAMI WITH MULTIPLE PEOPLE."

WITH THIS TREASURE, I SUMMON...

IT CAN'T BE—!

STOP!

KRNCH

GBM BHAM

SHF...

WAIT.

YOU STUPID JUJUTSU SORCERER!

WAKE UP!!

STOP MESSING AROUND!!

DAMMIT!

I HAVE URGENT BUSINESS TO DEAL WITH.

MASTER SUKUNA?

SEE YOU
LATER,
URAUME.

DON'T
NEGLECT
YOUR
PREPA-
RATIONS.

I SEE...

...

IT WON'T
BE MUCH
LONGER
UNTIL I'M
COMPLETELY
FREE.

UNDERSTOOD.

...

I SHALL
BE WAITING
FOR YOU.

FWSH

44

DON'T DIE.

THERE'S SOMETHING I NEED YOU TO DO.

PWOOM

QUIET.

UM...

...I NEED TO DEFEAT THE SHIKI-GAMI EVEN THOUGH I'M AN OUTSIDER.

IN ORDER TO KEEP FUSHI-GURO ALIVE...

JUST STAY THERE.

THE 2020 VALENTINES RANKINGS THAT I SERIOUSLY ALMOST FORGOT

RANKINGS (VALENTINES RECEIVED)	CHARACTER	AKUTAMI'S COMMENT
5 (19)	NANAMI	FIFTH IS FIRST.
6 (13)	KUGISAKI	NICE!
7 (7)	CHOSO	HE HASN'T BEEN SHOWING UP MUCH, HAS HE?
8 (6)	INUMAKI	EVEN THOUGH I'VE BARELY EXPLORED HIM...
9 (5)	MAKI	MAYBE I'LL CHANGE HER HAIRSTYLE...

THAT'S A SPECIALIZED BLADE FOR CURSED SPIRITS. THE SWORD OF EXTERMINATION.

IT'S ENVELOPED IN POSITIVE ENERGY, THAT IS SIMILAR TO REVERSE CURSED ENERGY.

KZZZ

IF I WAS A CURSED SPIRIT, I'D BE A GONER.

THUNK

KTNK

GRK
GRK
GRK...

WHAT'S NEXT?

SHp

ITS WOUNDS HAVE HEALED. IT DID SOMETHING...

55

NOT BAD!

KRMBL

KRK

FWM

MY
TURN.

FZZT...

GRAK

WHAM

...

IF I'M UNDER-
STANDING THIS
CORRECTLY,
IT'LL STAND UP...

JUST AS I THOUGHT.

KRRK

...THE SECOND WAS IMBUED WITH CURSED ENERGY.

UNLIKE THE FIRST ATTACK, WHICH WAS IMBUED WITH POSITIVE ENERGY...

THAT SECOND ATTACK...

IT'S SIMILAR TO YAMATA NO OROCHI.

BOTH OCCURRED AFTER THAT WHEEL ON ITS BACK TURNED.

AS FOR MY ATTACK... IT WAS ABLE TO RECOGNIZE DISMANTLE.

I BET THIS SHIKIGAMI'S POWER IS...

FURU'S INCANTATION OF THE TEN SACRED TREASURES AND THAT WHEEL REPRESENT A COMPLETE CYCLE AND HARMONY.

KIND OF LIKE A LATE THROW IN ROCK-PAPER-SCISSORS!

...THE ABILITY TO ADAPT TO ANY AND ALL PHENOMENA!

...IT MAY HAVE BEEN ABLE TO BEAT ME.

IF IT WAS ME FROM THAT TIME...

...MEGUMI FUSHI- GURO!

YOU'VE PIQUED MY INTEREST...

SHp

KEH KEH...

KEH KEH KEH.

DOMAIN EXPANSION...

THE 2020 VALENTINES RANKINGS THAT I SERIOUSLY ALMOST FORGOT

RANKINGS (VALENTINES RECEIVED)	CHARACTER	AKUTAMI'S COMMENT
10 (4)	INO	MAYBE THE INCIDENT WAS STARTING ABOUT THAT TIME?
11 (3)	IEIRI	MACROSS F IN A SET WITH GOJO.
	IJICHI	COME ON, TETSUO!
	KAMO	HE LOST TO CHOSO... HA HA!
14 (2)	MEI MEI	AGE INDETERMINATE.
	MIWA	AFTER ALL, SHE'S CUTE!
	OZAWA	EVEN THOUGH SHE JUST BRIEFLY POPPED IN?

SUKUNA HAS TWO TYPES OF SLASHING ATTACKS.

THE MAIN ATTACK IS DISMANTLE.

AND THE SECONDARY ATTACK, CLEAVE, CAN BE ADJUSTED DEPENDING ON THE TARGET'S TOUGHNESS AND CURSED ENERGY LEVEL TO CUT THEM DOWN IN ONE FELL SWOOP.

MALEVOLENT SHRINE DIFFERS FROM OTHER TYPES OF DOMAIN EXPANSION IN THAT IT DOESN'T CREATE A SEPARATE SPACE USING A BARRIER.

THE ABILITY TO REALIZE ONE'S INNATE DOMAIN WITHOUT USING A BARRIER IS AKIN TO AN ARTIST PAINTING A MASTERPIECE NOT ON A CANVAS, BUT IN THE AIR. A TRULY DIVINE TECHNIQUE.

...TO A MAXIMUM RADIUS OF NEARLY 200 METERS.

FURTHERMORE, BY ALLOWING AN ESCAPE ROUTE, A BINDING VOW IS FORMED, WHICH VASTLY INCREASES THE GUARANTEED HIT'S EFFECTIVE AREA...

TAKING MEGUMI FUSHIGURO INTO ACCOUNT...

...SUKUNA NARROWED THE EFFECT'S RANGE TO A 140-METER RADIUS ABOVE THE SURFACE.

*SFX: CLASH

STILL NO RECEPTION.

HOW'S YOUR PHONE?

BUT...I DON'T THINK WE NEED TO WORRY ANYMORE.

HUH?

IT'D BE BAD IF BOTH OF OUR PHONES RAN OUT OF POWER.

DON'T USE YOURS TOO MUCH, KEIKO.

ME NEITHER...

TRUE...

THAT MEGA-PHONE GUY IS HERE.

OH RIGHT, THAT G—

FOR INANIMATE OBJECTS— DISMANTLE.

FOR ANYTHING WITH CURSED ENERGY WITHIN RANGE—CLEAVE.

UNTIL MALEVOLENT SHRINE IS GONE...

...IT WILL RELENTLESLY ATTACK ALL TARGETS WITHIN THE EFFECTIVE RANGE OF ITS GUARANTEED HIT.

VWM

KRAK

...IS TO SLAUGHTER IT WITH A NEW ATTACK BEFORE IT CAN ADAPT.

THE ONLY WAY TO DEFEAT MAHORAGA...

CLEAVE FITS THE CRITERIA. HOWEVER...

KRAK

...BUT TO SLASHING ATTACKS IN GENERAL, THEN...

...IF IT HASN'T ADAPTED ONLY TO DISMANTLE...

82

BEGONE.

WHAT'RE YOU LOOKING AT?

THE MARKINGS UNDER SHIGEMO'S EYES INDICATE HOW MANY MIRACLES HE HAS STORED, BUT EVEN HE IS NOT AWARE OF THIS FACT.

LITTLE EVERYDAY MIRACLES ARE ERASED FROM SHIGEMO'S MEMORY AND STORED.

FOR EXAMPLE...

HEY! ALL THE SAME NUMBER!

4:44 44

ONCE AGAIN, I LIVE ...

THESE STORED MIRACLES ARE THEN RELEASED WHEN SHIGEMO'S LIFE IS IN DANGER.

HUH?

HIS LUCK HAD RUN OUT...

...IN HIS FIGHT AGAINST KENTO NANAMI.

NOT MUCH LONGER...

!

BLCH

!!

FWSH

FUSHI-GURO!

I THOUGHT I SAW ITADORI FOR A SECOND... OR WAS IT SUKUNA?!

THE 2020 VALENTINES RANKINGS THAT I SERIOUSLY ALMOST FORGOT

RANKINGS (VALENTINES RECEIVED)	CHARACTER	
17 (1)	OKKOTSU	SUKUNA
	PAPAGURO	HAIBARA
	PANDA	JUNPEI
	HANAMI	KAMO (NORITOSHI)

GENERAL COMMENT

WHAT ABOUT TODO?

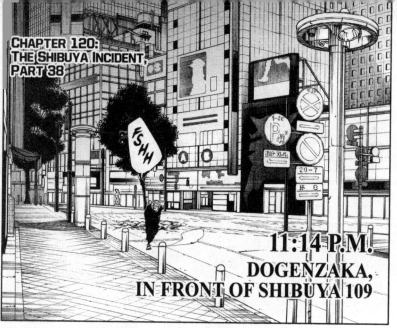

FSHH

11:14 P.M.
DOGENZAKA,
IN FRONT OF SHIBUYA 109

FSH...

TAKE A
GOOD
LOOK.

HEY,
BRAT.

HUFF!

HUFF!

"I'M WONDER-ING WHY THE HECK I HAVE TO BE EXECUTED."

JUST...DIE ALREADY.

BECAUSE OF YOU...

I NEED TO MOVE.

WITH HOW THINGS HAVE GONE...

...I'M NOTHING BUT A MURDERER.

I NEED TO FIGHT.

PHOTO ID

YEAH, MALAYSIA... KUANTAN WOULD BE NICE.

MALAYSIA...

GO THROUGH THEM PAGE BY PAGE... KINDA LIKE TAKING BACK THE TIME I'VE LOST.

FINALLY GET AROUND TO THE COUNTLESS BOOKS I'VE BOUGHT BUT NEVER READ.

BUILD A HOUSE ON A SECLUDED BEACH.

WHAT HAPPENED TO THEM...?

BUT WHAT ABOUT MAKI...AND NAOBITO?

YOU'RE HEADING OVER TO SAVE FUSHIGURO...

NO, RIGHT NOW YOU'RE...

I'VE DONE ENOUGH, HAVEN'T I?

YEAH, I'M JUST TIRED.

TIRED... SO TIRED.

COIN LOCKERS

I DIDN'T KNOW YOU WERE HERE...

WE'VE GOT HISTORY, AFTER ALL.

WANNA CHAT?

THE WHOLE TIME.

YUP.

I RAN. EVEN THOUGH I RAN AWAY, I CAME BACK WITH THE VAGUE REASON OF FINDING THE WORK WORTHWHILE.

WHAT WAS I TRYING TO DO ANYWAY?

HAIBARA...

NANA-MIN!

ITADORI.

IT'LL JUST END UP BECOMING A *CURSE* FOR HIM.

NO, HAIBARA, THAT'S NOT RIGHT. I CAN'T SAY THAT TO HIM.

ITADORI...

GETTING IT RIGHT!! LIMITLESS CURSED TECHNIQUE

• Now that the anime has begun, more people in Japan and overseas will check out *Jujutsu Kaisen*. Because of that, I can't keep bluffing my way through stuff. Yes, I'm talking about Gojo's cursed technique.

• So I asked my editor to find someone knowledgeable about mathematics for their input, and the inquiry in the *Jump* editorial staff turned up T-san, who has a master's degree in engineering (information geometry)!!

• I hope to share what I've learned in this volume and the next.

• I should've done this from the start!!

110

BODY REPEL!!

GNK GNK GNK

BODY REPEL—
SOUL MULTIPLICITY CREATES A REACTION DUE TO THE REJECTION OF FUSION. BY USING THIS EFFECT AND INCREASING THE SOUL'S ENERGY, THE OVER-WHELMING OUTPUT CAN BE DIRECTED AT AN OPPONENT.

SOUL MULTIPLICITY—
A TECHNIQUE THAT MERGES TWO OR MORE SOULS.

GRAK GRAK GRAK GRAK

BOO!

YOU ARE ME.

WHAT THE HELL?

SHNK

AAAGH!

'TIS JUST A CURSE SPOUTING NONSENSE.

GRK GRK

YEESH... NO NEED TO GET SO UPSET EVERY TIME.

BUT YOU KNOW WHAT?

ALL THAT BLABBERING...

YOU REALLY DON'T STOP TALKING.

I'LL MAKE SURE THOSE ARE YOUR DYING WORDS!

UNTIL YOU ACCEPT THAT FACT...

...THERE'S NO WAY YOU'LL EVER BEAT ME.

...A JUJUTSU SORCERER!

"YOU'VE GOT IT FROM HERE."

NANAMIN WOULDN'T LOSE HIS COOL.

NANA-MIN...

PROVE TO HIM THAT...

...I AM...

...YOU ARE...

I'LL STICK WITH MANIPULATING LIMBS, WHICH SHOULDN'T BE A PROBLEM TO SACRIFICE JUST LIKE A MOMENT AGO.

IDLE TRANSFIGURATION DOESN'T WORK ON ITADORI.

"I NEED TO FOCUS ON CONCENTRATING MY BODY'S FORM TO MAINTAIN TOUGHNESS"...

INCREASING MY SIZE BY MANIPULATING MY SOUL WOULD JUST MAKE ME A BIGGER TARGET. THAT MIGHT AS WELL BE SUICIDE.

消火栓

122

GETTING IT RIGHT!!
LIMITLESS CURSED TECHNIQUE ~INTRODUCTION~

T-SAN

EDITOR

AKUTAMI

T-SAN CAME TO MY WORKPLACE.

HM... I SEE...

...EXPLAINED IT LIKE THIS (IN THE GN BONUS CONTENT).

I READ THIS BOOK AND THEN...

TO BE CONTINUED IN VOLUME 15...

JUJUTSU

IT'S ALL WRONG!!

CHAPTER 122:
THE SHIBUYA INCIDENT,
PART 40

OHH... THAT WAS SCARY!

IF I TAKE A RISK AND MESS UP THE TIMING, I COULD END UP DEAD. I'LL STICK TO USING TRANSFIGURED HUMANS FOR NOW.

MWP
MWP
MWP

REDUCING RISK ISN'T THE ONLY REASON I'M USING TRANS-FIGURED HUMANS.

HE HAS MORE MOVES NOW.

DELAYED TRANS-FIGURATION, BODY DISMEMBER-MENT, AND MERGING...

!

DUN

IT'S DANGEROUS OVER THERE WITH ALL THOSE MONSTERS!

HEY, COME THIS WAY!

A STUDENT?!

TRY TO STAY SOMEW—

SORRY, BUT NOWHERE'S SAFE IN SHIBUYA.

WHERE'S MAHITO...?

UPSTAIRS!

134

GO AHEAD AND EAT WHATEVER'S IN THE WAY.

9:30 P.M.
SHIBUYA STATION B4F

DAGON.

DOWN THE HATCH!

MAHITOOO!

BWOOSH

11:16 P.M.
DOGENZAKA-KOJI

WASN'T THAT CRAZY?

I WAS JUST THERE.

DID YOU SEE THAT?

THE SPECIAL GRADE CURSED SPIRIT WHO'S BEEN CAUSING TROUBLE FOR OUR CLASS CLOWN?!

IT'S YOU, RIGHT?

!

PATCH-FACE...

...NOT TO LET HIM TOUCH ME...

THEY TOLD ME...

...SO YOU'LL HAVE TO AT LEAST LET ME SQUASH A FLEEING BUG LIKE YOU.

I THINK HIS CURSED TECHNIQUE HAS SOMETHING TO DO WITH THE SOUL...

I DON'T HAVE MUCH TO SHOW FOR TODAY...

SHK

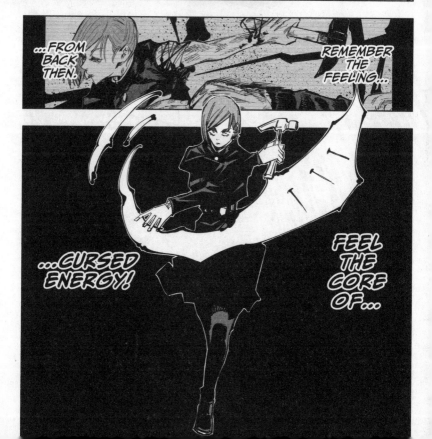

...FROM BACK THEN.

REMEMBER THE FEELING...

...CURSED ENERGY!

FEEL THE CORE OF...

144

DZZ
DZZ
DZZ

HAIRPIN!

SANP

WHAK
WHAK

NOT BAD. BUT...

HA HA HA!

I'LL BRING HER DEAD BODY TO YUJI ITADORI...

...AND DESTROY HIS SOUL!

...THAT WON'T WORK ON ME.

JUDGING BY THE WAY SHE TALKS...

...I'D SAY SHE'S A FRIEND OF HIS.

Extra Info

• Sukuna actually flew all the way outside the curtain in this scene.
• Since there was no particular effect on either Sukuna or Mahoraga and visually it had no particular bearing on the fight, I left it out.

DON'T DO IT, KUGISAKI!

NANAMI SAID SO TOO!

11:14 P.M.
SHOTO BUNKAMURA STREET
(OUTSIDE THE CURTAIN)

AND...WE DIDN'T TELL YOU SHOKO WAS HERE BECAUSE—

THE PARAMEDIC TEAM WAS PROBABLY LATE FOR THE SAME REASON.

BECAUSE YOU DIDN'T WANT ME DOING SOMETHING RECKLESS, RIGHT?

...WHILE THEY'RE STILL FIGHTING.

...I CAN'T JUST LEAVE...

EVEN SO...

CHAPTER 123: THE SHIBUYA INCIDENT, PART 41

JUJUTSU KAISEN

154

POP

SPLAT
SPLAT

CRAP, I—

KLINK

KLINK

KLINK

KLINK

KLINK
KLINK

VWUM

KRSH

I'M JUST A DOUBLE THOUGH.

HOW BORING.

SHE'S AVOIDING MY HANDS... THE 7:3 HAIRSTYLE SORCERER MUST HAVE WARNED HER!

I CAN CHANGE MY FORM LIKE THE ORIGINAL, BUT...

...I CAN'T MANIPULATE TRANSFIGURED HUMANS OR OTHER SOULS.

BWOOM

...FOR ME!

BUT THANKS FOR WEARING YOUR-SELF DOWN...

I'M NOT FIGHTING ITADORI. I CAN MANIPULATE MY FORM AS MUCH AS I WANT WITHOUT INCURRING RISKS.

THE FIRST ONE
RATTLED THE
NAILS TO MAKE
THEM POINT
UPRIGHT!

BUT WHAT DOES THAT MATTER?

...

I'VE BEEN THINKING ABOUT IT.

...THIS...

EVER SINCE I WAS TOLD ABOUT YOUR CURSED TECHNIQUE, I'VE THOUGHT...

!!

...WOULD BE EFFECTIVE AGAINST YOU.

SHE WAS BLUFFING TO MAKE IT SEEM LIKE SHE DIDN'T HAVE A PLAN!

BEFORE...

KUGI-SAKI?!

...TO STRIKE MAHITO'S SOUL VIA HIS BODY.

KUGISAKI USED RESO-NANCE...

AS A RESULT, RESONANCE WOULD RELAY FROM THE DOUBLE TO THE ORIGINAL'S SOUL.

FURTHER-MORE, THE DAMAGE DEALT TO THE ORIGINAL'S SOUL...

SPLACH

...WOULD THEN RE-BOUND...

...BACK TO THE DOUBLE!

YUJI ITADORI...

THIS CAN'T BE REAL!!

NO WAY!

...ISN'T MY ONLY...

...NATURAL ENEMY!

...DETONATE SOMEWHERE ELSE NEARBY.

I JUST FELT MY CURSED ENERGY...

HM... THAT'S WEIRD.

...YOU COULD'VE JUST GRABBED ME.

AND BACK THEN...

KREE

YOUR CURSED ENERGY ISN'T REALLY ALL THAT STRONG.

HOW DO I PUT THIS...

...SO YOU CAN'T USE YOUR CURSED TECHNIQUE, AM I RIGHT?!

YOU'RE LIKE A DOUBLE OR SOMETHING...

GRCHK

CORRECT...

A Nice Story

• Hiramatsu-san drew this design of a young Kugisaki for the anime, and I used it in the manga too.
• When Hiramatsu-san draws Kugisaki, she's actually cute.

CHAPTER 124:
THE SHIBUYA
INCIDENT,
PART 42

KUGI-
SAKI...?!

174

BWAM

THANK YOU!

GRCH

GRCH

GRCH

I COULDN'T
SAVE ANYONE.

I WASTED
EVERYONE'S
EFFORTS.

BUT...

THANK YOU FOR SHOWING ME THAT I'M NOT ALONE.

THAT'S WHY...

...I'M GONNA KILL YOU, HERE AND NOW!

KLNK

CORRECT...

THIS IS WHERE THE BATTLE REALLY BEGINS.

NOW THAT RESONANCE IS WORKING, THE ATTACKS SHOULD SLOW DOWN A BIT.

ACTU- ALLY...

TWITCH

WHAT ?!

I'M GONNA RUN AWAY!

!

DING DING

GET BACK HERE!

THWAK

FWUM

I COULD JUST IGNORE HIM AND HEAD STRAIGHT TO B5F, BUT I HAVE A FEELING LETTING HIM RUN LOOSE WOULD COME BACK TO BITE US LATER.

THE SUBWAY ...!

TWO MAHITOS?!

IS HE TRYING TO FUSE BACK TOGETHER TO HEAL?!

WAS THAT DOUBLE SOMEWHERE ELSE BEFORE?!

THEY WENT PAST EACH OTHER?! WHY...!!

?!

ITA-
DORI
...!

FURTHERMORE, DUE TO HER BATTLE AGAINST THE DOUBLE...

THE REAL BODY ACTED AS A BLIND SPOT SO THAT KUGISAKI WOULD NOT NOTICE THE SWITCH.

...SHE LET HER GUARD DOWN AGAINST MAHITO'S HANDS.

YOU'RE IN MY WAY!

NOW THEN...

KUGI- SAKI!!!

...WITH ONE TOUCH, BUT...

I COULDN'T KILL THE 7:3 HAIRSTYLE SORCERER...

...HOW ABOUT YOU?

2009...

GRAA-AHHH!! DIE!!

NOBARA KUGISAKI
(SIX YEARS OLD)

YOU HAFTA MAKE SURE TO GO FOR THE KILL WHEN THE OPPONENT IS RECOVERING.

MAYBE NEXT TIME, NOBARA.

TO BE CONTINUED

JUJUTSU KAISEN

reads from right to left, starting in the upper-right corner. Japanese is read from right to left, meaning that action, sound effects, and word-balloon order are completely reversed from English order.